D0498207

DOG TRICK OR CAT TREAT

PETS DRESS UP FOR HALLOWEEN

ECW Press

Published by ECW PRESS
2120 Queen Street East, Suite 200, Toronto, Ontario, Canada M4E 1E2

LIBRARY AND ARCHIVES CANADA CATALOGUING IN PUBLICATION

Klondike, Archie
Dog trick or cat treat : pets dress up for Halloween / Archie Klondike.

ISBN 978-1-55022-800-7

1. Dogs—Humor. 2. Cats—Humor. 3. Halloween costumes. 4. Dogs—Pictorial works. 5. Cats—Pictorial works. I. Title.

SF416.5.K56 2007   636.7002'07   C2007-903391-1

Cover Design: Tania Craan
Typesetting: Mary Bowness
Photo Research: Erin Press & Crissy Boylan
Printing: Paramount

This book is set in GoodDogCool

DISTRIBUTION
CANADA: Jaguar Book Group, 100 Armstrong Ave., Georgetown, ON L7G 5S4
UNITED STATES: Independent Publishers Group, 814 North Franklin Street, Chicago, Illinois, U.S.A. 60610

PRINTED AND BOUND IN HONG KONG

ECW PRESS
ecwpress.com

Shiloh

Chester Boots

Pug Rescue Halloween Parade

Tompkins Square Park Halloween Dog Parade, 2006

Piñta

Dobson

Sandy

Vinnie
and Milo

colby

Maki

Gabby

Merlijn de
Boze Tovenaar

American Visionary Arts Museum Pet Parade

Pug Rescue Halloween Parade

American Visionary Arts Museum Pet Parade

Tate

Tompkins Square Park Halloween Dog Parade, 2005

clover and cowboy

American Visionary Arts Museum Pet Parade

Mabel

Tompkins Square Park Halloween Dog Parade, 2005

Sir Alistair Pinklepurr Esquire

Daisy

cody

Buddha

Midnight

Spike

Tompkins Square Park Halloween Dog Parade, 2006

American Visionary Arts Museum Pet Parade

Thurston

Gracie

Belladonna

Tigger

Elsie MooCow

Tompkins Square Park Halloween Dog Parade, 2006

Ginger

American Visionary Arts
Museum Pet Parade

Patch

Lola and Mac Daddy

Pixie and Wicket

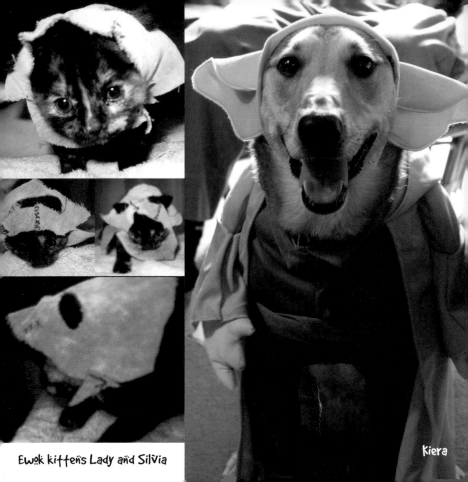

Ewok kittens Lady and Silvia

Kiera

Buddy

Teddy

CoCo

Bobo

Lyñdi Lu

Captain

old Man

Captain

Coco

Heidi

Coffee

Dax

Cleo

Tompkins Square Park
Halloween Dog Parade, 2005

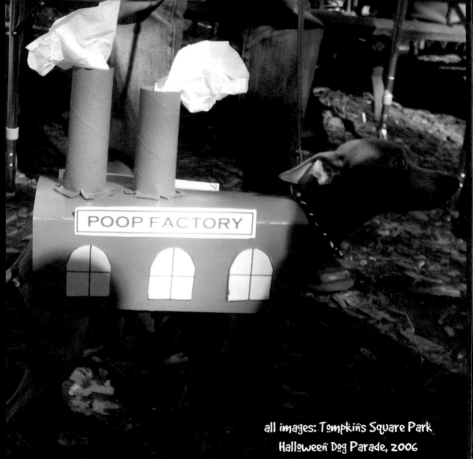

POOP FACTORY

all images: Tompkins Square Park
Halloween Dog Parade, 2006

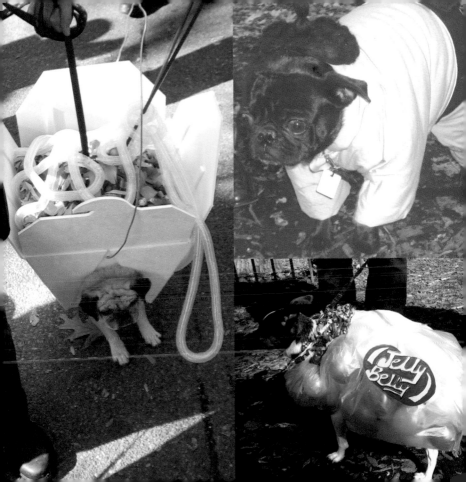

Carnevale di Venezia

Buddy

Maggie

Tompkins Square Park Halloween Dog Parade, 2006

Mac Daddy

Zoe-Grace

Daisy

Riley

Duke

Jue Yuň

Tompkins Square Park Halloween Dog Parade, 2005

Tompkins
Square Park
Halloween Dog
Parade, 2006

Napoleon

Photo credits

page 1 — "Darth Doggie" courtesy of Joanne (cover)
page 2 — "Chester Boots" courtesy of Andrea and Ted Williams
page 3 — "Sunshine Pug" courtesy of Catherine MacPhail
page 4 — "Lion Dog" courtesy of Ingemar VanBergen
page 5 — "Firefighter Pinta" courtesy of Michelle Runje
page 6 — "Dobson the Pumpkin" courtesy of J.R. Accettola (www.blackcats.org)
page 7 — "Sandy the Pink Fairy" courtesy of Gina Heitland
pages 8 and 9 — "Vinnie and Milo on the Hunt" courtesy of Michael McCusty and Valerie Valenzo
page 10 — "Colby Crustacean" courtesy of Jennifer Lockridge (cover)
page 11 — "Deputy Dawg" courtesy of Ken Berg (cover)
page 12 — "Cinderella Gabby" courtesy of Cindy Terrell
page 13 — "Merlijn" courtesy of Hilde Hayvaert
page 14 — "Monkey Puppy" courtesy of J. Gavin Heck
page 15 — "Firefighting Pug" courtesy of Catherine MacPhail (cover)
page 16 — "Patriotic Puppy" courtesy of J. Gavin Heck
page 17 — "Cowboy Tate" courtesy of Kim Preece
page 18 — "Skunk Dog" courtesy of Ingemar VanBergen
page 19 — "Clover and Cowboy" courtesy of Shutterjo
page 20 — "Canine Royalty" courtesy of J. Gavin Heck
page 21 — "Tequila Kitten" courtesy of Teresa MacLellan and Drew Haines
page 22 — "Robin Dog" courtesy of Ingemar VanBergen
page 23 — "C/batman" courtesy of Erin Nicole Smith
page 24 — "Wonder Pug" courtesy of Steven Rockarts
page 25 — "Super Cody" courtesy of Cindy Terrell
page 26 — "Little Devil Dog" courtesy of Ingemar VanBergen (left); "Little Devil Buddha" courtesy of Jill N. Hamilton-Krawczyk (top right); "Midnight Angel" courtesy of Monica Leone (middle right & cover); "Spike the Devil" courtesy of Susan Szews (bottom right)
page 27 — "Angel/Devil" courtesy of J. Gavin Heck
page 28 — "Ribbit Meow" courtesy of Michael Rose
page 29 — "Powderpuff Fairy" courtesy of Amy Lane
page 30 — "Chiquita" courtesy of Carolyn Kinniery
page 31 — "Bella the Cat" courtesy of Heather Bailey
page 32 — "Tigger Frog" courtesy of Jennifer Lockridge
page 33 — "Quack" courtesy of Susan Szews (cover)
page 34 — "Dessert Dog" courtesy of Ingemar VanBergen

page 35 — "Hot Dog Dog" courtesy of JRotunda85
page 36 — "Independence Dog" courtesy of J. Gavin Heck
page 37 — "Elvis at Rest" courtesy of Melissa Madsen
page 38 — "Bride and Groom" courtesy of Billie (The Mad Dog & Billie Show)
page 39 — "Pixie Princess and Wicket Monster" courtesy of Chris Pirillo
page 40 — "Ewok Kittens" courtesy of Melanie Larson; "Yoda Pup" courtesy of Ken Berg
page 41 — "Buddy Vader" courtesy of Lisa Percival (cover)
page 43 — "Frog Dog" courtesy of Liz Kearley
page 43 — "Coco the Bee" courtesy of Meighan Makarchuk
page 44 — "Count Bobala" courtesy of Rick Catlow
page 45 — "Chief Hound" courtesy of Carolyn Whiteside
page 46 — "Pilot, Sweater, and Pumpkin" courtesy of Alan and Stefanie Baker (top row); "Wigged-out Witch Cat" courtesy of Meighan Makarchuk (bottom left); "Kitten in a Bonnet" courtesy of Margaret and Patrick Press (bottom right)
page 47 — "Bumble Cat" courtesy of Sarah Poon (top); "Ladybug" courtesy of Rosio Hernandez (bottom left); "Rawr" courtesy of Melanie Larson (bottom right)
page 48 — "Gryffindog" courtesy of Ingemar VanBergen
page 49 — "Bobo the Japanese Salary Man" courtesy of Rick Catlow
pages 50 and 51 — "Sumo Pug," "Jelly Belly," "Poop Factory," "Take-Out Pug" all courtesy of Ingemar VanBergen
page 52 — "Carnevale Princess" courtesy of Claude@Munich (flickr.com/people/c-s-n/)
page 49 — "Birthday Buddy" courtesy of Lisa Percival
page 54 — "Maggie the Cheercat" courtesy of Mary-Margaret Schmidt
page 55 — "SpideyDog" courtesy of Ingemar VanBergen
page 56 — "Daddy Mac" courtesy of Billie (The Mad Dog & Billie Show — top left); "Zoe-Grace" courtesy of Carl Patmore (top right); "DinoPug" courtesy of Steven Rockarts (bottom left); "FrankenPug" courtesy of Lauren Debreceni (bottom right)
page 57 — "BumblePug" courtesy of Bret Robertson
page 58 — "Little Red Riding Hood" courtesy of Betty Lee (cover)
page 59 — "Spider" courtesy of Ingemar VanBergen
page 60 — "Happy Bee" courtesy of Ingemar VanBergen
page 61 — "Napoleon" courtesy of Ashley Proper
cover — "Rocco" courtesy of Amy Lane (front flap bottom)